INTRODUCTION

I dedicate this **BOOK** to our **CREATOR** of **THIS BEAUTIFUL** and **WONDERFUL UNIVERSE** and to all the languages of this **EARTH.**

Meaning of God :

The perfect and all-powerful spirit or being that is worshipped especially by Christians, Jews, and Muslims as the one who created and rules the universe. A being conceived as the perfect, omnipotent, omniscient originator and ruler of the universe, the principal object of faith and worship in monotheistic religions.

Brahman – 1. Relating to Brahman or the Creator or the Supreme Spirit

[The creator and ruler of the universe and source of all moral authority; the supreme being].

John-4: KJV

24. God is a Spirit: and they that worship him must worship him in spirit and in truth.

Acts-17: KJV

24. God that made the world and all things therein, seeing that He is Lord of heaven and earth, dwelleth not in temples made with hands;

1 John-4: KJV

12. No man hath seen God at any time. If we love one another, God dwelleth in us, and His love is perfected in us.

Genesis-11: KJV

1. And the whole earth was of one language, and of one speech.
4. And they said, Go to, let us build us a city and a tower, whose top may reach unto heaven; and let us make us a name, lest we be scattered abroad upon the face of the whole earth.

[The sin made them to think foolishly that they can reach GOD by building a tower up to Heaven]

Genesis-11: KJV

9. Therefore is the name of it called Babel; because the LORD did there confound the language of all the earth: and from thence did the LORD scatter them abroad upon the face of all the earth.

The Tower of Babel, a classic symbol of language diversification

Our world is becoming more and more globalized by the day, and as a result, many of us are being introduced to a variety of some of the most spoken languages in the world. It's not surprising that there are more than 7,000 widely spoken languages in the world.

In 2023, there were around 1.5 billion people world wide who spoke English either natively or as a second language,

slightly more than the 1.1 billion Mandarin Chinese speakers at the time of survey.

Hindi and Spanish accounted for the third and fourth most widespread languages that year.

How GOD is called in different LANGUAGES:-

Afrikaans / Dutch –God; **Amharic**-Agzer, Agzibeher; **Arabic** –Allah; **Breton** –Dew; **Chinese**-Shang Di; **Cornish**-Dyw; **Czech**-Buh,Hospodin; **Estonian**-Jumal; **Fijian**-Kalou; **Finnish** – Jumala; **French**-Dieu; **German**-Gott; **Greenlandic**- Guuti, Naalagaq; **Hebrew** -Elohim (eh-lo-him); **Icelandic**- Gu, Drottinn, Himnasmiur; **Bahasa Indonesia**- Allah; **Tuhan**- Bapa , Abba, Father; **Italian**- Dio; **Indian** languages - "DEV, Bhagwan, Swami, etc.

Sanskrit - देवः Deva, ईश्वरः īśvara;
Bengali-bhogoban/ishwar/debota/probhu;
Jamaica- Jah; **Japanese**- Kami, Tentei, Tenshu,
Shinmei; **Lithuanian** – Dievas; Multilingual-Jehova;
Norwegian – Gud; **Russian** – bog; **Romanian**-
Dumnezeu; **Spanish**-Dios; In Urdu (**India and
Pakistan**) and Farsi (**Iran**) = Khuda; **uzbek**-
Olloh,Hudo,Tangri; **welsh** – Duw; **Zulu**- Nkos;

Acts-2: KJV

**11. Cretes and Arabians, we do hear them speak
in our tongues the wonderful works of God.**

**[But one language we all understand is 'LOVE'
This is not the love that stands for passion, but
for <u>COMPASSION</u>].**

Psalm111:4. KJV

*He hath made His wonderful works to be
remembered: the LORD is gracious and full of
compassion.*

1Corinthians13:GN.

*1.I may be able to speak the languages of
human beings and even of angels, but if I have
no love, my speech is no more than a noisy
gong or a clanging bell.
2. I may have the gift of inspired preaching; I
may have all knowledge and understand all*

secrets; I may have all the faith needed to move mountains - but if I have no love, I am nothing.

34. "A new commandment I give unto you, That ye love one another; as I have loved you, that ye also love one another."

34. "O give thanks unto the LORD; for he is good; for his mercy endureth for ever."

28. Blessed are they that hear the word of God, and keep it.

<u>PREFACE</u>

<u>*Psalms-14: KJV*</u>

2. *"The LORD looked down from heaven upon the children of men, to see if there were any that did understand, and seek God."*

<u>*1 Chronicles-16:10 KJV*</u>

Glory ye in His holy name: let the heart of them rejoice that seek the LORD.

[This book is-compiled briefly from THE HOLY-BIBLE- choosing some appropriate verses mentioned in 'THE SCRIPTURE' about our CREATOR'S -1). Creation, how sin entered and its consequences, 2). GOD'S anger, when the chosen people drifted away from HIM. 3). <u>CREATOR'S </u>everlasting love-towards HIS creation.

[How will you know about 'GOD-THE CREATOR' of this Universe]

<u>*John-5:*</u> KJV

39. *"Search the scriptures; for in them ye think ye have eternal life: and they are they which testify of me."*

<u>*Romans-10:*</u> KJV

14. *"How then shall they call on Him in whom they have not believed? and how shall they*

believe in Him of whom they have not heard? and how shall they hear without a preacher

Romans-10: KJV

15. "And how shall they preach, except they be sent? as it is written, How beautiful are the feet of them that preach the gospel of peace, and bring glad tidings of good things!".

When the animals can recognize their owner, why not we human beings who are gifted with six senses (know about) recognize our MASTER-'THE CREATOR' of this Universe.

Isaiah-1:

3. "The ox knoweth his owner, and the ass his master's crib: but Israel doth not know, my people doth not consider."

[What is the need to know HIM?

Jeremiah-22: KJV

16. "He judged the cause of the poor and needy; then it was well with him: was not this to know me? saith the LORD."

Romans-10: KJV

13. "For whosoever shall call upon the name of the Lord shall be saved."

Proverbs-25: KJV

25. As cold waters to a thirsty soul, so is good news from a far country.

<u>KNOW YOUR CREATOR-</u>

<u>ALMIGHTY GOD</u>

[Many times either we have less time or no time to know about our CREATOR, who created this BEAUTIFUL UNIVERSE].

Revelation-1: KJV

8. "*I am Alpha and Omega, the beginning and the ending, saith the Lord, which is, and which was, and which is to come, the Almighty.*"

{Man says, 'show me I BELIEVE', GOD SAYS, "BELIEVE ME - I WILL SHOW YOU"}

Matthew-5: KJV

8. Blessed are the pure in heart: for they shall see God.

{We human beings should recognize and acknowledge the beauty of GOD'S creation. There is no creation without A CREATOR}. [The name '<u>GOD</u>' belongs to HIM alone].

Job-37: KJV

5. <u>God</u> *thundereth marvellously with His voice; great things doeth He, which we cannot <u>comprehend</u>.*

Genesis-1: KJV

1. "In the beginning God created the heaven and the earth."

[ALMIGHTY GOD, executed His creation in six days and rested on the seventh day-it is the Sabbath- the day to remember and honour 'THE CREATOR' of this Universe.]

Exodus-20: KJV

11. For in six days the LORD made heaven and earth, the sea, and all that in them is, and rested the seventh day: wherefore the LORD blessed the sabbath day, and hallowed it.

Surah- [10]- Yunus

 (2) Lo! your Lord is Allah Who created the heavens and the earth in six Days, then He established Himself upon the Throne, directing all things.

Genesis-2: KJV

1. Thus the heavens and the earth were finished, and all the host of them.

Psalms-19: KJV

1. The heavens declare the glory of God; and the firmament sheweth His handywork.

13. Mine hand also hath laid the foundation of the earth, and my right hand hath spanned the heavens: when I call unto them, they stand up together.

12. He hath made the earth by His power, He hath established the world by His wisdom, and hath stretched out the heavens by His discretion.

11. He hath made everything beautiful in His time: also He hath set the world in their heart, so that no man can find out the work that God maketh from the beginning to the end.

22. It is He that sitteth upon the circle of the earth, and the inhabitants thereof are as grasshoppers; that stretcheth out the heavens as a curtain, and spreadeth them out as a tent to dwell in:

28. Hast thou not known? hast thou not heard, that the everlasting God, the LORD, the Creator of the ends of the earth, fainteth not, neither is weary? there is no searching of His understanding.

39. *Know therefore this day, and consider it in thine heart, that the LORD He is God in heaven above, and upon the earth beneath: there is none else.*

[HE planned and executed beautifully this Universe, where we got the summary of HIS execution in the first two chapters of 'GENESIS' of 'THE HOLY BIBLE'].

18. *For thus saith the LORD that created the heavens; God Himself that formed the earth and made it; He hath established it, He created it not in vain, He formed it to be inhabited: I am the LORD; and there is none else.*

26. *And God said, Let us make man in our image, after our likeness: and let them have dominion over the fish of the sea, and over the fowl of the air, and over the cattle, and over all the earth, and over every creeping thing that creepeth upon the earth.*

7. And the LORD God formed man of the dust of the ground, and breathed into

*his nostrils the breath of life; and man became
a living soul.*

<u>Genesis-2: KJV</u>

*16. And the LORD God commanded the man,
saying, Of every tree of the garden thou mayest
freely eat:*

*17. But of the tree of the knowledge of good
and evil, thou shalt not eat of it: for in
the day that thou eatest thereof <u>thou
shalt surely die</u> .*

*22. And the rib, which the LORD God had taken
from man, made He a woman, and brought her
unto the man.*

*23. And Adam said, This is now bone of
my bones, and flesh of my flesh: she shall
be called Woman, because she was taken out
of Man.*

<u>Deuteronomy-30: KJV</u>

**15. See, I have set before thee this day life and
good, and death and evil.**

<u>1 Chronicles 16: KJV</u>

**12. Remember His marvellous works that He
hath done, His wonders, and the judgments of
His mouth;**

[We are all created with a purpose and plan by
'THE CREATOR' of this Universe. We have to

connect with Him continually for our spiritual and moral well being, which is very important for the human race to strive and thrive].

1 Chronicles 16: KJV
8. *"Give thanks unto the LORD, call upon His name, make known His deeds among the people."*
11. *"Seek the LORD and His strength, seek His face continually."*

Revelation-14: KJV
7. Saying with a loud voice, Fear God, and give glory to HIm; for the hour of His judgment is come: and worship Him that made heaven, and earth, and the sea, and the fountains of waters.

Jeremiah-10: KJV
10. But the LORD is the true God, He is the living God, and an everlasting king: at His wrath the earth shall tremble, and the nations shall not be able to abide His indignation.

[There is only one scripture [given by our CREATOR through HIS chosen prophets] We are not supposed to add or subtract anything to GOD'S words].

30. Therefore, behold, I am against the prophets, saith the LORD, that steal my words everyone from his neighbour.

32. What thing so ever I command you, observe to do it: thou shalt not add thereto, nor diminish from it.

18. For I testify unto every man that heareth the words of the prophecy of this book, If any man shall add unto these things, God shall add unto him the plagues that are written in this book.

5. Every word of God is pure: He is a shield unto them that put their trust in Him.
6. Add thou not unto His words, lest He reprove thee, and thou be found a liar.

2. Ye shall not add unto the word which I command you, neither shall ye diminish ought from it, that ye may keep the commandments of the LORD your God which I command you.

[History of sin, how it entered the world through 'satan the devil' –'the deceiver'

**9. And the great dragon was cast out ,
that old serpent, called the Devil, and Satan,
which deceiveth the whole world: he was
cast out into the earth, and his angels were
cast out with him.**

*1. Now the serpent was more subtil than
any beast of the field which
the LORD God had made. And he said unto
the woman, Yea, hath God said, Ye shall
not eat of every tree of the garden?
2. And the woman said unto the serpent, We
may eat of the fruit of the trees of the garden:
3. But of the fruit of the tree which is in the
midst of the garden, God hath said, Ye shall not
eat of it, neither shall ye touch it, lest ye die.*

[Our 'CREATOR' says, 'For in the day that thou
eatest thereof 'thou shalt surely die'].
[Whereas the deceiver satan says, 'you will not
die'].

*4.And the serpent said unto the woman, Ye shall
not surely die:*

[Adam and Eve disobeyed GOD. Because of this
disobedience, the curse came on man-kind],
<u>The sin entered the human-race:-</u>

Romans-5: KJV

**12. "Wherefore, as by one man sin entered into
the world, and death by sin; and so death
passed upon all men, for that all have sinned:"**

1Peter-5: KJV

**8. "Be sober, be vigilant; because your
adversary the devil, as a roaring lion, walketh
about, seeking whom he may devour:"**

Isaiah-14: KJV

**12. How art thou fallen from heaven, O Lucifer,
son of the morning! how art thou cut down to
the ground, which didst weaken the nations!**

Genesis-6: KJV

**5. And GOD saw that the wickedness of man
was great in the earth, and that every
imagination of the thoughts of his heart
was only evil continually.**

Matthew-15: KJV

**19. For out of the heart proceed evil thoughts,
murders, adulteries, fornications,
thefts, false witness, blasphemies:
20. These are the things which defile a man:**

Deuteronomy-24: KJV"The

16. _The fathers shall not be put to death for the children, neither shall the children be put to death for the fathers:_ **every man shall be put to death for his own sin.**

[Our iniquities (pride, evil thoughts, disobedience, etc.) have separated us from 'THE LIVING GOD-CREATOR-THE ALMIGHTY']

Isaiah-59: KJV

2. But your iniquities have separated between you and your God, and your sins have hid His face from you, that He will not hear.

Jeremiah-6: KJV

19. "Hear, O earth: behold, I will bring evil upon this people, even the fruit of their thoughts, because they have not hearkened unto my words, nor to my law, but rejected it."

Isaiah-59: KJV

4. None calleth for justice, nor any _pleadeth_ **for truth: they trust in vanity, and speak lies; they conceive mischief, and bring forth iniquity.**

Jeremiah-9: KJV

5. And they will deceive everyone his neighbour, and will not speak the truth: they have taught their tongue to speak lies, and weary themselves to commit iniquity.

6. Thine habitation is in the midst of deceit; through deceit they refuse to know me, saith the LORD.

Psalm-10: KJV

4. The wicked, through the pride of his countenance, will not seek after God: God is not in all his thoughts.

Proverbs-16: KJV

18. Pride goeth before destruction, and an haughty spirit before a fall.

[In the Old-Testament time, people had to give sacrifice for their sins. When people were not feeling sorry for their sins, they started sacrificing useless animals].

Deuteronomy-15: KJV

21. And if there be any blemish therein, as if it be lame, or blind, or have any ill blemish, thou shalt not sacrifice it unto the LORD thy God.

Deuteronomy-17 KJV

1. Thou shalt not sacrifice unto the LORD thy God any bullock, or sheep, wherein is blemish, or any evil favouredness: for that is an abomination unto the LORD thy God.

8."And if ye offer the blind for sacrifice, is it not evil? and if ye offer the lame and sick, is it not evil? offer it now unto thy governor; will he be pleased with thee, or accept thy person? saith the LORD of hosts."

11. To what purpose is the multitude of your sacrifices unto me? saith the LORD: I am full of the burnt offerings of rams, and the fat of fed beasts; and I delight not in the blood of bullocks, or of lambs, or of he goats.

13. Bring no more vain oblations; incense is an abomination unto me; the moons and sabbaths, the calling of assemblies, I cannot away with; it is iniquity, even the solemn meeting.

14. Your new moons and your appointed feasts my soul hateth: they are a trouble unto me; I am weary to bear them.

15. And when ye spread forth your hands, I will hide mine eyes from you: yea, when ye make many prayers, I will not hear: your hands are full of blood.

16.Wash you, make you clean; put away the evil of your doings from before mine eyes; cease to-do evil;

Proverbs-21: KJV

3. To do justice and judgment is more acceptable to the LORD than sacrifice.

Isaiah-61: KJV

8. For I the LORD love judgment, I hate robbery for burnt offering; and I will direct their work in truth, and I will make an everlasting covenant with them.

Ecclesiastes-5: KJV

1. Keep thy foot when thou goest to the house of God, and be more ready to hear, than to give the sacrifice of fools: for they consider not that they do evil.

Isaiah-29: KJV:

13. Wherefore the Lord said, For as much as this people draw near me with their mouth and with their lips do honour me, but have removed their heart far from me, and their fear toward me is taught by the precept of men:

Matthew-15: KJV

9. But in vain they do worship me, teaching for doctrines the commandments of men..

[To deliver us from the bondage of sin, our CREATOR first gave us the 'TEN COMMANDMENTS' [laws /statutes] Deautronomy-5, HE is the GOD who sees the

HEART. We cannot live our life the way we like by breaking the laws given by HIM].

Leviticus 26: KJV

3. *"If ye walk in my statutes, and keep my commandments, and do them;"*
4. *"Then I will give you rain in due season, and the land shall yield her increase, and the trees of the field shall yield their fruit."*

Deuteronomy-11: KJV

18. *"Therefore shall ye lay up these my words in your heart and in your soul, and bind them for a sign upon your hand, that they may be as frontlets between your eyes."*

Leviticus 26: KJV

14. *"But if ye will not hearken unto me, and will not do all these commandments;"*
20. *"And your strength shall be spent in vain: for your land shall not yield her increase, neither shall the trees of the land yield their fruits."*

Jeremiah-21: KJV

8. *And unto this people thou shalt say, Thus saith the LORD; Behold, I set before you the way of life, and the way of death.*
14. *But I will punish you according to the fruit of your doings, saith the LORD: and I will kindle a*

fire in the forest thereof, and it shall devour all things round about it.

20. For there shall be no reward to the evil man; the candle of the wicked shall be put out.

[THE CREATOR of this Universe is against idol-worship, especially by the people-called chosen one (Israel) who melt HIS heart with their cry, when they were under the bond of slavery. He rescued them to show HIS LOVE.]

23. And it came to pass in process of time, that the king of Egypt died: and the children of Israel sighed by reason of the bondage, and they cried, and their cry came up unto God by reason of the bondage.

6. Wherefore say unto the children of Israel, I am the LORD, and I will bring you out from under the burdens of the Egyptians, and I will rid you out of their bondage, and I will redeem you with a stretched out arm, and with a great judgments:

[The CREATOR'S anger was, the people whom He loved, drifted away from HIM. The Israel,

continually murmured provoking HIM and went
behind the imagination of their heart making
idols, worshiping them].

Isaiah-1: KJV

2. *Hear, O heavens, and give ear, O earth: for
the LORD hath spoken, I have nourished and
brought up children, and they
have rebelled against me.*

Isaiah-30: KJV

1. *Woe to the rebellious children, saith the
LORD, that take counsel, but not of me; and that
cover with a covering, but not of my spirit, that
they may add sin to sin:*

Exodus-32: KJV

8. *They have turned aside quickly out of the way
which I commanded them: they have made
them a molten calf, and have worshipped it, and
have sacrificed thereunto, and said, These be
thy gods, O Israel, which have brought thee up
out of the land of Egypt.*

Isaiah 2: KJV

8. *Their land also is full of idols; they worship
the work of their own hands, that which their
own fingers have made:*
9. *And the mean man boweth down, and the*

*great man humbleth himself: therefore forgive
them not.*

Habakkuk-2: KJV

**18. What profiteth the graven image that the
maker thereof hath graven it; the molten image,
and a teacher of lies, that the maker of his work
trusteth therein, to make dumb idols**

Deuteronomy-5: KJV

**8. Thou shalt not make thee any graven image,
or any likeness of anything that is in heaven
above, or that is in the earth beneath, or that is
in the waters beneath the earth.**

[It is blasphemy to call the imaginary idols-
GOD. The name 'GOD' belongs only to 'THE
CREATOR' of this Universe.

Deuteronomy-5: KJV

7."Thou shalt have none other gods before me."

Deuteronomy-13 KJV

**11. And all Israel shall hear, and fear, and shall
do no more any such wickedness as this is
among you.**

Isaiah-42: KJV

**8. I am the LORD: that is my name: and my glory
will I not give to another, neither my praise to
graven images.**

15. But if ye will not obey the voice of the LORD, but rebel against the commandment of the LORD, then shall the hand of the LORD be against you, as it was against your fathers.

20. And He said, I will hide my face from them, I will see what their end shall be: for they are a very froward generation, children in whom is no faith.

15. And they shall know that I am the LORD, when I shall scatter them among the nations, and disperse them in the countries.

[We cannot make images of our imagination and call them God. Imagination is a 'lie' created by the 'liar-the devil' to deceive and destroy the plans of GOD. [The devil acts in such a way, blinding the conscience of human-beings making them insensitive to sin].

22. *For my people is foolish, they have not known me; they are sottish children, and they have none understanding: they are wise to do evil, but to do good they have no knowledge.*

12. I will smite them with the pestilence, and disinherit them, and will make of thee a greater nation and mightier than they."

19. And they shall go into the holes of the rocks, and into the caves of the earth, for fear of the LORD, and for the glory of His majesty, when He ariseth to shake terribly the earth.

22.Cease ye from man, whose breath is in his nostrils: for wherein is he to be accounted of?

9. And He said, Go, and tell this people,
Hear ye indeed, but understand not;
and see ye indeed, but perceive not.
10. Make the heart of this people fat, and make
their ears heavy, and shut their eyes; lest
they see with their eyes, and hear with
their ears, and understand with
their heart, and convert, and be healed.

20. The anger of the LORD shall not return, until He have executed, and till He have performed the thoughts of His heart: in the latter days ye shall consider it perfectly.

[THE CREATOR is-ALMIGHTY GOD. We His creation should not divide and distribute HIS 'power' to the idols made out of sinful hands and give praise and worship to those imaginary idols].

Leviticus-26: KJV

1. Ye shall make you no idols nor graven image, neither rear you up a standing image, neither shall ye set up any image of stone in your land, to bow down unto it: for I am the LORD your God.

Exodus-20: KJV

5. Thou shalt not bow down thyself to them, nor serve them: for I the LORD thy God am a jealous God, visiting the iniquity of the fathers upon the children unto the third and fourth generation of them that hate me:

Jeremiah 7: KJV

8. Behold, ye trust in lying words, that cannot profit.

9. Will ye steal, murder, and commit adultery, and swear falsely, and burn incense unto Baal, and walk after other gods whom ye know not;

Hosea-4: KJV

6. My people are destroyed for lack of knowledge: because thou hast rejected

knowledge, I will also reject thee, that thou shalt be no priest to me: seeing thou hast forgotten the law of thy God, I will also forget thy children.

Deuteronomy-11: KJV

16. Take heed to yourselves, that your heart be not deceived, and ye turn aside, and serve other gods, and worship them;

17. And then the LORD'S wrath be kindled against you, and He shut up the heaven, that there be no rain, and that the land yield not her fruit; and lest ye perish quickly from off the good land which the LORD giveth you.

Isaiah-2: KJV

12. For the day of the LORD of hosts shall be upon every one that is proud and lofty, and upon every one that is lifted up; and he shall be brought low:

18. And the idols He shall utterly abolish.

Deuteronomy-11 KJV

26. Behold, I set before you this day a blessing and a curse;

27. A blessing, if ye obey the commandments of the LORD your God, which I command you this day:

**28. And a curse, if ye will
not obey the commandments of the LORD
your God, but turn aside out of the way which I
command you this day, to go after other gods,
which ye have not known.**

Jeremiah-12: KJV

*17. But if they will not obey, I will utterly pluck
up and destroy that nation, saith the LORD.*

[GOD gave HIS instructions to the prophets, to
instruct the people through Scripture with lots
of dos and don'ts].

Exodus-23: KJV

*21. Beware of Him, and obey His voice, provoke
Him not; for He will not pardon your
transgressions: for my name is in Him.*

Isaiah-5: KJV

*20. Woe unto them that call evil good, and good
evil; that put darkness for light, and light for
darkness; that put bitter for sweet, and sweet
for bitter!
21. Woe unto them that are wise in their own
eyes, and prudent in their own sight!*

Isaiah-9: KJV

16. For the leaders of this people cause them

to err; and they that are led of them are
destroyed.

17. Therefore the Lord shall have no joy in their
young men, neither shall have mercy on their
fatherless and widows: for everyone is
an hypocrite and an evildoer, and
every mouth speaketh folly. For all this
His anger is not turned away, but His hand is
stretched out still.

Isaiah 1: KJV

4. "Ah sinful nation, a people laden with iniquity,
a seed of evildoers, children that are corrupters:
they have forsaken the LORD, they have
provoked the Holy One of Israel unto anger, they
are gone away backward."

Jeremiah-11: KJV

14. Therefore pray not thou for this people,
neither lift up a cry or prayer for them: for I will
not hear them in the time that they cry unto me
for their trouble.

Jeremiah-15: KJV

6. Thou hast forsaken me, saith the LORD, thou
art gone backward: therefore will I stretch out
my hand against thee, and destroy thee; I am
weary with repenting.

Isaiah-1: KJV

3.The ox knoweth his owner, and the ass his master's crib: but Israel doth not know, my people doth not consider.

Ezekiel-18: KJV

30. Therefore I will judge you, O house of Israel, every one according to his ways, saith the Lord GOD. Repent, and turn yourselves from all your transgressions; so iniquity shall not be your ruin.

Jeremiah-12: KJV

10."Many pastors have destroyed my vineyard, they have trodden my portion under foot, they have made my pleasant portion a desolate wilderness."

Jeremiah-23: KJV

1. Woe be unto the pastors that destroy and scatter the sheep of my pasture! saith the LORD.

[GOD, fights for His children, who obey Him, by keeping His laws].

Isaiah-59: KJV

1. Behold, the LORD'S hand is not shortened, that it cannot save; neither his ear heavy, that it cannot hear:

Exodus-15: KJV

3.The LORD is a man of war: the LORD is His name.

11. And I saw heaven opened, and behold a white horse; and He that sat upon him was called Faithful and True, and in righteousness He doth judge and make war.

29. For our God is a consuming fire.

24. For the Lord thy God is a consuming fire, even a jealous God.

43. Therefore say I unto you, The kingdom of God shall be taken from you, and given to a nation bringing forth the fruits thereof.

1. Hear the word of the LORD, ye children of Israel: for the LORD hath a controversy with the inhabitants of the land, because there is no truth, nor mercy, nor knowledge of God in the land.

7. Let the wicked forsake his way, and the unrighteous man his thoughts: and let him return unto the LORD, and He will

have mercy upon him; and to our God, for He will abundantly pardon.

[GOD hates rituals, He wants our heart to be right with HIM].

Hosea-6: KJV

6. *For I desired mercy, and not sacrifice; and the knowledge of God more than burnt offerings.*

Proverbs15: KJV

8. *The sacrifice of the wicked is an abomination to the LORD: but the prayer of the upright is his delight.*

Jeremiah-23: KJV

24. Can any hide himself in secret places that I shall not see him? saith the LORD. Do not I fill heaven and earth? saith the LORD.

Isaiah-55: KJV

6. *"Seek ye the LORD while he may be found, call ye upon him while he is near:"*

Jeremiah-32: KJV

27. Behold, I am the LORD, the God of all flesh: is there anything too hard for me?

1 Samuel-16: KJV

7. But the LORD said unto Samuel, Look not on

his countenance, or on the height of his stature; because I have refused him: **"for the LORD seeth not as man seeth; for man looketh on the outward appearance, but the LORD looketh on the heart."**

Micah-6: KJV

8. He hath shewed thee, O man, what is good; and what doth the LORD require of thee, but to do justly, and to love mercy, and to walk humbly with thy God?

Psalms-103: KJV

8. The LORD is merciful and gracious, slow to anger, and plenteous in mercy.
9. He will not always chide: neither will He keep His anger for ever.
11. For as the heaven is high above the earth, so great is His mercy toward them that fear Him.

Isaiah-54: KJV

8. In a little wrath I hid my face from thee for a moment; but with everlasting kindness will I have mercy on thee, saith the LORD thy Redeemer.

2 Chronicles-7: KJV

14. If my people, which are called by my name, shall humble themselves, and pray, and seek my face, and turn from their wicked ways; then will

I hear from heaven, and will forgive their sin, and will heal their land.

Deuteronomy-30 KJV

3. That then the LORD thy God will turn thy captivity, and have compassion upon thee, and will return and gather thee from all the nations, whither the LORD thy God hath scattered thee.

Jeremiah-9: KJV

**23. Thus saith the LORD, Let not
the wise man glory in his wisdom, neither let
the mighty man glory in his might, let not
the rich man glory in his riches:
24. But let him that glorieth glory in this, that
he understandeth and knoweth me, that I am
the LORD which exercise loving kindness,
judgment, and righteousness, in the earth: for in
these things I delight, saith the LORD.**

Isaiah-2: KJV

**17. And the loftiness of man shall be
bowed down, and the haughtiness of men shall
be made low: and the LORD alone shall
be exalted in that day.**

[The need to KNOW OUR CREATOR, to understand the meaning of life and for a peaceful co-existence we have to follow the manual [word of GOD] or we are in great trouble].

9. "Blessed are the peacemakers: for they shall be called the children of God."

12. And now, what doth the Lord thy God require of thee, but to fear the Lord thy God, to walk in all His ways, and to love Him, and to serve the Lord thy God with all thy heart and with all thy soul.

28. Observe and hear all these words which I command thee, that it may go well with thee, and with thy children after thee forever, when thou doest that which is good and right in the sight of the LORD thy God.

3. Who forgiveth all thine iniquities; who healeth all thy diseases;
4. Who redeemeth thy life from destruction; who crowneth thee with lovingkindness and tender mercies.

19."And I will give them one heart, and I will put

a new spirit within you; and I will take the stony heart out of their flesh, and will give them an heart of flesh:"

20."That they may walk in my statutes, and keep mine ordinances, and do them: and they shall be my people, and I will be their God."

[GOD IS HOLY and PERFECT, HE IS THE LIVING GOD- THE ALMIGHTY-THE CREATOR of this universe].

{CREATOR wants and expects from us [His creation] to be like HIM Holy and Perfect because He created us in HIS image}.

Leviticus-20: KJV

7."Sanctify yourselves therefore, and be ye holy: for I am the LORD your God."
26. "And ye shall be holy unto me: for I the LORD am holy, and have severed you from other people, that ye should be mine."

Matthew-5: KJV.

48. Be ye therefore perfect, even as your Father *which is in heaven is perfect.*

Deuteronomy-14: KJV

2. For thou art an holy people unto the LORD thy God, and the LORD hath chosen thee to be a peculiar people unto himself, above all the nations that are upon the earth.

40. *That ye may remember, and do all my commandments, and be holy unto your God.*

6. And shewing mercy unto thousands of them that love me, and keep my commandments

43. **"Whoso is wise, and will observe these things, even they shall understand the lovingkindness of the LORD."**

3. And one cried unto another, and said, Holy, holy, holy, is the LORD of hosts: the whole earth is full of His glory.

29. Give unto the Lord the glory due unto His name: bring an offering, and come before Him: worship the LORD in the beauty of holiness.

11. For from the rising of the sun even unto the going down of the same my name shall be great among the Gentiles; and in every place incense shall be offered unto my name, and a pure

offering: for my name shall be great among the heathen, saith the LORD of hosts.

Isaiah 45: KJV

22."Look unto me, and be ye saved, all the ends of the earth: for I am <u>God</u>, and there is none else."

Romans 14: KJV

11."For it is written, As I live, saith the Lord, every knee shall bow to me, and every tongue shall confess to God."

Proverbs 3: KJV

5. Trust in the LORD with all thine heart; and lean not unto thine own understanding.
6."In all thy ways acknowledge Him, and He shall direct thy paths."

Psalm-34: KJV

8. O taste and see that the LORD is good: blessed is the man that trusteth in Him.

Psalm-91: KJV

15. He shall call upon me, and I will answer him: I will be with him in trouble; I will deliver him, and honour him.

13. Let us hear the conclusion of the whole matter: Fear God, and keep His commandments: for this is the whole duty of man.

8. Finally, be ye all of one mind, having compassion one of another, love as brethren, be pitiful, be courteous:

11. Thine, O LORD, is the greatness, and the power, and the glory, and the victory, and the majesty: for all that is in the heaven and in the earth is thine; thine is the kingdom, O LORD, and thou art exalted as head above all.

12. Both riches and honour come of thee, and thou reignest over all; and in thine hand is power and might; and in thine hand it is to make great, and to give strength unto all.
13. Now therefore, our God, we thank thee, and praise thy glorious name.

14. "For this God is our God forever and ever: He will be our guide even unto death".

<u>*END NOTE*</u>

[Gospel of New-Testament is the fulfilment of 'The Prophecy' of Old-Testament].
The sacrifice of '<u>THE CREATOR</u>' of this great Universe is revealed through HIS only begotten son <u>JESUS CHRIST</u> by obeying and offering Himself as the final sacrifice to redeem us from the clutches of sin. This will be explained in my next book '<u>BEYOND CHRISTMAS</u>'.

www.ingramcontent.com/pod-product-compliance
Lightning Source LLC
Chambersburg PA
CBHW040116150726
48005CB00013B/1732

9798893635386